GOD'S
WORD
FOR
YOU

GOD'S
WORD
FOR
YOU

DICK MILLS

Whitaker House

GOD'S WORD FOR YOU

Dick Mills Ministries, Inc.
P.O. Box 2600
Orange, CA 92859

ISBN: 0-88368-273-7
Printed in the United States of America
Copyright © 1973 by Whitaker House

Whitaker House
30 Hunt Valley Circle
New Kensington, PA 15068

7 8 9 10 11 12 13 14 15 16 / 06 05 04 03 02 01 00 99 98 97

CONTENTS

FOREWORD

For my part, Dick Mills' character, ministry in the Word of God and prophetic gift continue to define the kind of ministry we should expect of a contemporary prophet to the Body of Christ.

His scripturally-centered style and his submissiveness of spirit are the fountainhead of the authority with which he ministers. I commend him to you, and rejoice in the seasons of refreshing this book will bring to many.

Jack W. Hayford, D.Litt.
Senior Pastor
The Church On The Way
Van Nuys, California

"And when he had spoken unto me, I was strengthened…" Daniel 10:19

A WORD FROM THE LORD
FOR THE HAGGARD BUSINESSMAN

> *The man diligent in his business
> shall not waste his time on non-
> entities.* (Proverbs 22:29, paraphrased)

Watch a man who is diligent in his business.
  Observe his skill.
  Observe his speed.

If he is a wicked man, do not allow yourself to envy
his prosperity. Never resent the gains and promo-
tions of an unbeliever. Do not allow your heart to
be filled with resentment when you see wrong
prospering. Look to me.

I have a plan for your life.
  A plan of blessing,
  a plan of advancement,
  a plan by which you can succeed,

11

a plan enabling you to develop
in the school of faith.

But learn what you can from the wicked: be skillful in the time of apathy, unconcern and indifference. Apply yourself so that whatever you set your hand to do will be done with all your might.

Not only be skillful, but be swift.
My whole program is one of action

                              and motion
                              and energy
                              and outreach.

The angels move rapidly. Even My Son constantly moved about, doing good. So be sure to develop not only your skill, but your use of time. Then you will be a unique person, having a proficiency at utilizing your talent and displaying your gift.

I am manifesting Myself in you. I have given you these talents to use for My glory and My honor. You are going to be fruitful and productive. You are going to be contented with that which I bring forth in your life. You are going to be satisfied with
your lot,
your station,
your position,
your faith.

12

You will not waste time on nonessentials. My blessing will give you a sense of fulfillment and achievement which will bring gratification of heart and rejoicing of soul.

I have spoken it, I will also bring it to pass. (Isaiah 46:11)

A WORD FROM THE LORD
FOR THE HURRIED BUSINESSMAN

> ... *ye shall not go out with
> haste, nor go by flight** . . . *The
> Lord will go before you.* (Isaiah
> 52:12)

I know your schedules.
I know your responsibilities.
I know the decisions you must make.
I know the pressures which are upon you.

Because of your activities, because of the schedules
and the deadlines, you are caught in the momentum
of motion which robs you of your inward strength,
your inward reservoir, your inward peace.

Be not hasty or impulsive.
Be not impetuous or impatient.
I can work a miracle inside you that will give you
an internal calm, serenity and peace even while

14

you are busy in your employment. Then you will be
enabled to meet your schedules and deadlines and
make your decisions rightly.

Do not go with haste. If you go with compulsion
because of pressures upon your own soul, you are
then stifling your own creativity, and hindering
your own individuality. You are stopping the flow
of My blessings.

Here is where you are of value—here is where your
true worth appears: when My Spirit is released
within you and flows through you. Then your life
 becomes fruitful
 becomes refreshing
 becomes invigorating
 becomes stimulating
 becomes challenging
 becomes rewarding.

If you become over-anxious and begin to be motivated by guilty fear, or because of compulsions,
you cannot be at your best.

Be still,
and know that I am God
within you.

You must have your times of waiting before Me.
You must have your quiet times of drawing
strength. Then when you go forth, you will go with

assurance and confidence. You will have an inward reservoir, an inward reserve of strength that shall sustain you in the most hurried of situations.

Hath He spoken, and shall He not make it good?
(Numbers 23:19)

A WORD FROM THE LORD
FOR THE HASSLED BUSINESSMAN

> *When a man's ways please the*
> *Lord, he maketh even his enemies*
> *to be at peace with him.* (Prov-
> erbs 16:7)

When a man's ways please Me, I Myself will deal
with all others who oppose him. I will divert the
antagonism of all competitors and opponents. I
will keep My hand on all those who would stand in
his way to impede his progress.

Your only concern must be
to seek first My kingdom.
Then all these things
will be added to you.

I have given you My laws of sowing and reaping. I
have given you the principle that if you sow sparingly, you will reap sparingly; if you sow bounti-

fully, you will reap bountifully. Are you distressed in the competitive struggle? Sow much faith in Me. Trust in My promises. Seek my face. Do my will. The very faith that you sow will produce a great harvest of reward.

I know the ruthlessness of modern man.
I know the underhanded business tactics.
I know the unethical practices.
I know when you are victimized and intimidated
    because of your faith in Me.

Promotion does not come from man.
It comes from Me.

I, the Lord, have put My hand upon you. I have raised you up for this very reason, that I might show My power in you.

Though the heathen rage,
    though the people imagine a vain thing,
        though they take counsel against you,
            though they plan your destruction,
            yet, because your ways please Me, I will
            protect you. I will lift you above the power-
            struggles, when you find yourself caught in
            the crossfires of ambitious climbers, pushy
            promoters and people who are using their
            positions as stepping-stones to higher posi-
            tions.

18

I will give you an immunity so that you will not be caught in the turmoil of struggling which goes on within the breasts of worldly men.

I will deal with the competition.
I will silence the opposition.
I will cause your enemies to be at peace with you.

You will do your work under the protection of My hand. You will be kept at your post of duty until My purposes have been fulfilled. No man, by his own design, can move you, hurt you or destroy you.

Because your ways please Me, you shall be secure in your post of duty.

Stand still, and see the salvation of the Lord. (Exodus 14:13)

A WORD FROM THE LORD
FOR THE HUSTLING BUSINESSMAN

> *In the morning go to work; in*
> *in the evening don't let up. You*
> *know not when success will come,*
> *either morning or evening.*
> **(Ecclesiastes 11:6, paraphrased)**

I have given you time as a gift.

Whether you succeed or whether you fail depends upon what you do with the time I have given you. I know the tremendous responsibilities you are facing, and the decisions you are constantly making. I am not removed from the pressures of the business world.

You must remember that when I was here I was surrounded by working people
business people
professional people.

20

One of My followers was a tin merchant.
One of My followers was a tax collector.
Many of My followers were commercial fishermen.
I had followers who were students.
I had followers who mended nets.
I had followers who worked in the fields.
I had followers who knew responsibility,
                    who knew decision,
                    who knew how important it is
                        to properly utilize time.

This is what I am saying to you:
  I am interested in your success.
  I am interested in your character development.
  I am interested in your happiness and blessing.
  This is why I teach you of time.

I will show you how to save time, if you will seek
My face, turn to My Word and draw near to Me. I
will even show you how to save your funds and
manage your finances. I will cause you to make the
most of your time, so that you are not doing that
which is non-productive and that which is fruitless.

I will show you how to save your energy so that
you are not merely running for the sake of running, returning from your day exhausted, without
having achieved your goal.

I will show you how to save your funds so that you will not be putting your money into a bag with holes in it.

With My help, wisdom and guidance,
with Me directing the affairs of your life,
you can prosper in the wise expenditure of your time, energy and funds.

Therefore, be sure to keep busy.
But busy as I direct you and lead you.
Then you shall see My blessings overtaking you.

The Lord shall fight for you, and ye shall hold your peace. (Exodus 14:14)

A WORD FROM THE LORD
FOR THE HARRIED BUSINESSMAN

> *Come ye yourselves apart into*
> *a desert place, and rest a while.*
> (Mark 6:31)

You must come apart for a time of rest

a time of refreshing
a time of renewal
a time of waiting
on Me.

You have been caught in a whirlpool of activity which has fatigued you. You have been engulfed in your business activities, and have become weary. You have faced the threat of reverses because of fluctuating conditions. There hangs over your head the threat of loss because of an uncertain economy. You have been anxious concerning your future.

This pressure upon you has caused a fatigue to come

    to your soul
    to your spirit
    to your mind
    to your body.

I am calling you to come apart.

This will not take days and days of leisure. Nor will it take weeks or months. I am doing a quick work in the earth. I will give you the ability to come apart from your business, your activities, your pressures, your stresses and strains. I will show you how to be quickly invigorated, stimulated, inspired and refreshed.

I will touch you.

I will renew your strength.
I will give you a change of pace.
I will give you a fresh breath.
I will give you new directions.
I will give you new incentives and objectives.

It is in the quiet time, in the stillness, even in the time of change, that I will manifest Myself to you.

You shall be as a runner who has paused long enough to get his second breath, his second wind.

Then you shall go forth with new strength
                    new courage
                    new enthusiasm.

You shall continue on, fulfilling your responsibilities, doing your duties, working at your place of labor— but with My hand having touched you. Having come apart and rested awhile, you shall then go forth to higher heights, deeper depths and greater blessings in the days that lie ahead of you.

> *The effect of righteousness [is]*
> *quietness and assurance forever.*
> (Isaiah 32:17)

A WORD FROM THE LORD
FOR THE BEREAVED

> ... *the righteous is taken away*
> *from the evil to come.* (Isaiah
> 57:1)

You have lost a loved one.

Many anxious thoughts are crowding into your soul.
The very shock of bereavement finds you unpre-
pared. You are re-living many memories. You are
thinking recurring thoughts from the past. Anxieties and apprehensions crowd in with all manner
of uncertainties.

Within your soul is one great question:

"Why?"

"Why did the Lord allow this?"
"To what purpose is this?"

But you must remember that I have declared Myself to be the First and the Last
the Alpha and the Omega
the same, yesterday, today and forever.

This is an interval of time. A milepost. A phase of your life. This is not the end of your life. This is not the last. My purposes are being realized. My will is being done in earth, as it is in Heaven.

I have said in My Word, "The righteous are taken away from the evil to come." Little do you know how your loved one was spared, and kept from the difficulties of the future. I saw the times of testing, the times of temptation, the times of tribulation. In My divine wisdom, knowing what was best, I removed that loved one. You must say with courage, "As for God, His way is perfect."

Furthermore
I add to My heavenly numbers as it pleases Me.

There are many functions in the City of Light.
There are many activities in the Heavenly City.

Many times, I reach into the earth

and bring a soul here
because of a need which exists here.

I have singers.
I have the joyous ones.
I have the praisers.
I have happy people.
This city is populated with people of MY CHOICE.
I HAVE CHOSEN to bring your loved one home.

    But yours is an unfinished task.
    The very fact that you are left shows that you
have an earthly task which remains yet to be accomplished.

So be not given to grief.
Do not let mourning hang over you as a cloud.

Look to Me.

I will reveal My will to you.
I will show you your unfinished task.
I will give you the courage and composure
   to do the very thing I have called you to do.

Your task will be fulfilled through faith
                     through integrity
                     through persistence
                     through determination.

Then I will bring you to My Great City, and you will share in My joy.

> *I shall go to him, but he shall
> not return to me.* (II Samuel
> 12:23)

29

A WORD FROM THE LORD
FOR THE LONELY

> *You will not be forgotten by*
> *Me, says the Lord.* (Isaiah 44:
> 21, paraphrased)

You are all alone and forlorn.

This has been forced upon you by a chain of events
over which you have no control. There is now a
void within you.

You have been deprived of the companionship
                  the fellowship
                  the blessing
                      of having many friends and
                      loved ones about you.

But you must rise above your loneliness.
I have a higher position for you.

Instead of this cloud of gloom being over you— instead of your spirit being depressed within you and anxious moments coming— instead of apprehension concerning your own future and security, I would have you rise above your loneliness, and put it under your feet as a footstool.

Rise above it all
rather than sit in a room with gloomy thoughts, depressing memories and anxious concerns.
All these merely feed your self pity, keep you submerged, hinder you from finding your place in the sunshine.

Flee to Me
> for strength
> for comfort
> for guidance
> for direction.

As I stretch forth My hand of power, bringing you out of your loneliness, you will again return to fruitful activity. You will reach out and touch others who have needs.

I know your loneliness.
You must remember that I sat over a city of thousands, and wept alone. There was none with Me. My grief, my anguish, my concern was for the well-being of others, and their failure to accept My love, My compassion, My forgiveness.

I know you by name.
I have watched the decisions you have made.
I have seen the disappointments as they came to
you.
I know where you have been hurt.
I know the very ones who have caused the hurt.

But this is all for a purpose:
  that in your brokenness, a fragrance may come
  forth which will make
    someone else's load a little lighter
    someone else's path a little brighter
    someone else's song a little happier
    someone else's day a little more cheery.

That which has happened to you is for My purpose:
that you might understand suffering humanity—
that you might be able to relate to human problems— that you might be able to tell others that I
LIVE, and that I am available to those who call
upon Me.

Thus
  you will be a channel of blessing.
  You will be an outflowing river of refreshment.

As My Spirit is released within you, flowing out
and touching those who are grieving and mourning in emptiness, shallowness and loneliness, you

will rejoice because you have found your appointed place under the sun.

Can a mother forget her little child and not have love for her own son? Yet even if that should be, I will not forget you. (Isaiah 49:15, Living Bible)

A WORD FROM THE LORD
FOR THE DISCOURAGED

> *. . . David encouraged himself*
> *in the Lord his God.* (I Samuel
> 30:6)

My word to you is to rise above your discouragement
    at once.

Lay it aside
as a tattered garment which is to be cast off and
discarded.

Discouragement has kept you down, has submerged you, has kept you downtrodden and has
robbed you of the confidence you need to face the
future.

I am not capricious.

Your discouragement has not come from Me.
I have not even permitted it.

Your discouragement has come because, in your
reasonings, you have rationalized the answers to
your problems— you have mentally resolved many
pressures and have leaned to your own understanding— you have maneuvered and manipulated with
self-effort, taking things into your own hands.

But all of this came to nothing
because I was not in it.

These were not My plans; they were your plans.
These were not My ideas; they were your ideas.

Not only are you aware that your plans have failed
to materialize, but you are bearing the weariness of
   striving,
   struggling,
   trying beyond human energy
     to produce achievement and fulfillment.

This has not materialized, and you are frustrated
in spirit. But rather than admit that your plans
have failed— plans which you produced without
My wisdom and My guidance— you have permitted a wave of bewilderment and discouragement to come to you. It has submerged you like a
rising tide.

You must turn to Me at once.

You must look to Me for direction. By My Word and by My Spirit, I will give you a word of wisdom and a word of knowledge. As you seek Me, I will grant to you the gift of faith to believe for even that which is impossible.

As My Word came to Jonah the second time, even so you shall approach your same problems a second time. But you will see them in a different light. You will see them in MY light.

My wisdom shall prevail.
My strength shall overcome.
My victory shall be yours.
My power shall be displayed.

You shall come forth in triumph, rejoicing in My great goodness, rejoicing in My ability to take your poor efforts which neither materialized nor succeeded, and re-direct them in channels of divine assistance.

With My help, you shall see victory.
Your soul will rejoice within you.
Your life will be free.
Your energy will be boundless.

"It is not by might,

nor by power,
but by My Spirit."

*Why art thou cast down, O my Soul? . . . hope
thou in God.* (Psalms 42:5)

A WORD FROM THE LORD
FOR THE RESTLESS

> *How lightly you gad about,*
> *changing your way!* (Jeremiah 2:36, RSV)

Oh, restless spirit, be still!
Oh, restless spirit, be calm!

Turmoil, agitation and unrest are driving you relentlessly. You are being robbed of many blessings. You have hastened on in great speed. You have run until you have become weary of running.

Your anxieties have been as an obsession urging you on. You have no peace,
> no tranquillity,
> no joy,
> no security.

Your thoughts are anxious thoughts.
Your attitudes are those of turmoil.
Your plans are agitated plans.

You have no foundation of stability under you. You are moving as a restless one from place to place, not knowing that for which you search, always, always reaching for that which is elusively out of reach.

"Be still and know that I am God!"
Stand still and see My salvation!

I have many things to speak to you about— but you are so restless and moving so rapidly that you are not taking time to sit down and converse with Me.

I have many things to show you— but your eyes cannot look in My direction. Your attention has been diverted to the shifting sands of the earth and the changing tides.

I have many gifts in My treasury which I would give you, which would enhance your life,
                              enrich your life,
                              augment your life,
                              give meaning to your life,
                              give purpose to your life.

But you are running . . . .

39

Therefore
I cannot give you these gifts.
You are unreceptive.

So I say to you,
Reconsider—knowing that I have promised to
lead you beside still waters. Turn to Me with all
your heart. Let My healing hand touch you, and
I will deliver you from turbulence,

agitation,

turmoil,

conflict,

restlessness.

You will be transformed by My mighty power into
a channel of blessing—calmness—composure—
tranquility—and quietness.

You will be as a sign and a wonder to those who
knew you in your previous restless state. It will be
as a complete surprise to them when they see what
I am doing in you.

Your soul will be satisfied, for you will learn to
drink deeply from My wells.

[Your] strength is to sit still. (Isaiah 30:7)

A WORD FROM THE LORD
FOR THE PERFECTIONIST

> ... *my chosen shall long enjoy*
> *the word of their hands.* (Isaiah
> 65:22, RSV)

Stop punishing yourself.
Stop driving yourself.
Stop pushing yourself
   relentlessly.

You must begin to enjoy the good blessings I have
given you. I have given you health and security. I
have provided for you and given you talents. I
have given you a sphere of influence. I have given
you a ministry. I have a work for you to perform.

Yet you do not enjoy that which I have given you.

Within you is a mechanism which punishes you,

41

a mechanism which does not allow you joy, nor happiness, nor contentment.

Neither will you allow others ever to rest in contentment. You do not allow those with whom you work to be at ease. You have a striving obsession.

You feel
you cannot stop
to take a look around
and beyond yourself.

You cannot enjoy My handiwork. You have a feeling of guilt which will not let you enjoy leisure time, nor take time off for renewal, refreshment and reviving.

You have driven yourself
but I have not driven you.

You have pushed yourself beyond the limits of human endurance—but I am not pushing you.

I would have you enjoy
the works of My hands,
the home I have given you,
the family I have given you,
the surroundings I have given you,
your friends,
your loved ones,
and fellow believers.

Therefore, My word to you is:
  Do not punish yourself.
  Do not drive yourself.
  Do not approach life in a fury.
  Rest in Me.

Understand that only that which is done by Me
has any lasting value. If I do it, there is nothing
you can add to it— nothing you can take away.

You have been deprived of much inward contentment and happiness because you would not allow
yourself to enjoy
the very things
I have given you.

  My people shall be satisfied with my goodness.
  (Jeremiah 31:14)

A WORD FROM THE LORD
FOR THE IMPERFECTIONIST

> *The Lord is able to give thee*
> *much more than this.* (II Chroni-
> cles 25:9)

You begin many tasks—
  but seldom finish any.

You begin with enthusiasm—
  but your enthusiasm soon wanes.

Your life has consisted of starting in many channels, but not following through in any of them.

Consequently, you have looked at yourself, and
have been hounded with
          imperfections,
          incompleted tasks,
          starts never finished,
          programs never consummated,

ideas never carried through,
plans never fulfilled.

You are hiding behind a fatigue of unfinished work
—and the weariness of having so much to do, yet
not having enough time to get all things done.

There is something better
than being wearied
by incompleted jobs
    unfinished tasks
       unending pursuits which do not lead to comple-
         tion or fulfillment.

I am able
to give you much more than this.

I am able
to give you purpose,
            meaning,
                objectives,
                   goals,
                incentives,
            and orientation.

I will perfect that which concerns you. My purpose is to fulfill and complete that which I have
begun in your life. I, who have called you, will be
faithful to do it.

Therefore, know this:
 Instead of weariness,
 instead of fatigue,
 instead of the exhaustion which goes with half-
    done tasks, unfinished jobs and incomplete la-
    bor— I will divert your energies and your ef-
    forts into channels of completion and fulfill-
    ment.

Your tasks will be completed one at a time, and
your life will evolve into a sequence of perfect
completion and accomplishment.

This will be your joy—
this will be your blessing:
 You shall no longer be fatigued with the weariness of a life unfulfilled. Your soul shall rejoice
 as you behold Me bringing to perfection that
 which I have begun in your life.

*Better is the end of a thing than the begin-
ning* .... (Ecclesiastes 7:8)

A WORD FROM THE LORD
FOR THE AGGRESSORS

> *. . . seekest thou great things*
> *for thyself? seek them not.* (Jer-
> emiah 45:5)

This is My word to you:
  I am not trying to destroy your ambitions.
  Neither am I trying to destroy your aggressions.
  But they must be properly channeled.

You have a driving force within you. This force
does not want to stop until it has achieved success. Therefore your life is busied

with plotting,
with planning,
with manuevering.

I see all this.
I would have you understand that in seeking great

things for yourself, you are being motivated by self-love.

I would not deprive you of success.
Nor would I rob you of prosperity.
But I am a jealous God.
I will not share My glory with another.
  The blessings which I have for you
    will not only enrich and enhance your life,
    but they will show forth My praises.

In your seeking,
in your determination,
in your aggressions,
  your motives have been tainted with self-seeking
  and self-love. This is a form of self-worship.

I demand that you worship Me.
I expect you to worship Me.
I demand all praise.

I will not permit My praises to be offered to graven images. Therefore I ask you to stop and search your heart. Commit your way to Me, and do not lean to your own understanding.

  Allow Me to scrutinize the inner recesses of your heart. Allow me to analyze,
                inspect,
                  look closely at your motives.

I will bring you to a place of understanding.
I will bring you to a place of wisdom.
I will bring you to a place of knowledge.
You will then see how to channel your determinations, your incentives and your aggressions *for My glory.*

I am not trying to kill your spirit.
I am not trying to rob you of your driving forces.
I only want them harnessed
for My glory
and My honor
so that I can use you fully.

All that is done in your life must be for My glory, and not for your own aggrandizement.

Are you seeking great things for yourself?
Seek them no longer.
Are you seeking great things for Me?
Seek them with all your heart.

I will help you determine between that which is for My glory, and that which is for yours. With keen discretion, you will be able to discard that which is for your glory. You will cling to that which is for My glory, and all your energies will be used to extend My kingdom.

Your soul and your spirit will stand uncondemned;

you will be able to say, "This is the Lord's doing; to Him be the glory."

Wherefore do ye spend money for that which is not bread? (Isaiah 55:2)

A WORD FROM THE LORD
FOR THE NON-AGGRESSORS

> ... *it is time to seek the Lord.*
> (Hosea 10:12)

It is time to seek My face.
I desire to come and pour you out a blessing.

You have been passive.
You have rested in smug complacency.
You have not exerted yourself.
You have not shown determination
  to win heaven's prize.

I have many rewards for those who press forward
and seek the prize. But in your passiveness, you
have allowed unconcern to envelop you.

You have become inactive.
You are making no effort.

In skepticism and unbelief, you wonder why—
  why your life has been so fruitless—
  why you have not seen the supernatural—
  why the miraculous power of God has been hidden.

I will tell you why:
  Your own unconcern,
  your own indifference,
  your own passivity
    robs you of heaven's prize.

Therefore, it is time to re-kindle the flame of devotion. It is time to set your heart to seek Me.

It is time to arise from indifference, unconcern, apathy and lukewarmness.

It is time to realize that
  prizes are available for the persistent;
  blessings are available for the determined;
  victories can be accomplished by the fervent;
  prayers will be answered for the energetic.

You are to love Me sincerely:
  emotionally, with all your soul;
  intelligently, with all your mind;
  energetically, with all your heart.

You must arise *now*.
You must cast off the garments of complacency.

You must put on the garments of praise.
You must begin to seek Me.

Then, I, the Lord, will bow the heavens and come down. I will envelop you in My love. I will encircle you with My power. I will thrust you forth in My energy. You will see signs and wonders performed in My name, saith the Lord of Hosts.

Neglect not the gift that is in thee . . . . (I Timothy 4:14)

A WORD FROM THE LORD
FOR THE COMPETITORS

> ... *we wrestle not against flesh*
> *and blood, but against* ... *spir-*
> *itual wickedness in high places.*
> (Ephesians 6: 12)

Your tests are not with people.
People are not your enemies.
Your vision has been blurred.

Instead of fighting the good fight of faith— instead of realizing that the contest of life is between light and darkness—
    your attention has been diverted to people;
    you have come in conflict with people;
    you have contested with people;
    you are competing with people.

But I say to you, This is a fight of faith. You

cannot fight this battle by maneuvering with strategy and human cleverness, trying to outwit people.

This fight has two opposing poles:
> light and darkness,
> right and wrong,
> good and evil,
> God and Satan.

Therefore,
> put on the whole armor I provide, and begin to fight the good fight of faith.

You are not wrestling with flesh and blood.
Your enemies are not human beings.
Your competitors are not people.

The warfare is between ideologies: the spirit of truth and the spirit of error.

The warfare is between philosophies: earthly materialism and heavenly treasure.

The warfare is between two eternal dwelling places: Heaven and hell.

Therefore, do not engage in conflict with people.
Your warfare is not on the human level. It is
> against principalities and powers,

against the rulers of this world,
against spiritual wickedness in high places,
against Satan.

Satan is trying
to destroy the souls of men;
You are called to win those souls to Me.

Satan is trying
to delude and deceive men's minds.
Your calling is to bring them to the mind of Christ.

Satan is trying
to divert men's attention from righteous paths.
Your calling is to illuminate those paths and make
   them so plain that many shall walk therein.

Take your eyes off people.
They are not your enemies.
They are not your competition.
You have a much greater foe.

Your victories will be much greater when you recognize your real foe. Then you will be able to win
   in My name,
      by the power of My Word,
         using the strength,
            the power,
               the force that I give.

If you compete against people,
and temporarily win,
you will have no lasting satisfaction.

But
when you see the powers of darkness shaken,
the powers of evil vanquished,
the power of the enemy put to flight,
My name vindicated,
My truth proclaimed,
My people released,
then truly you will say, "The battle is the Lord's."

Stand still, and see My salvation. I will fight for you, and you will hold your peace.

Do good unto all men, especially unto them who are of the household of faith. (Galatians 6:10)

A WORD FROM THE LORD
FOR THE NON-COMPETITORS

> *The children of Ephraim, being
> armed, and carrying bows, turned
> back in the day of battle.* (Psalms
> 78:9)

You became a believer
>>> because you needed fellowship,
>>>> because you needed forgiveness
>>>>> because you wanted to have a faith.

You have enjoyed
>>> the fellowship
>>> the music
>>> the joy
>>> the happiness
>>> the freedom
>>> the forgiveness
>>> My sunshine

My presence
My blessings.

Now you have found that there is a price which
must be paid to be a believer. You have been
drawn into the great battle which exists between
life and death.

You have found that many believers are unpopular
and unaccepted. You have discovered that their
philosophies, their attitudes and their faith are not
accepted. You have found that society does not
sanction the separated life of the believer.

You have found that the believer is faced with ridi-
cule and rejection by friends and foes. You have
found that there is a warfare.

Now you are withdrawing.

You are trying to avoid the conflicts,
                              the commitment,
                              the contest.

You would like to abide in My garden
    where it is fragrant,
                    refreshing,
                    stimulating
                    and invigorating.

But you have no desire for the encounter. Therefore, you have withdrawn from the real battle. You have retreated from the good fight of faith. You have failed to put on My whole armor. You are not being a soldier for Me.

This has caused two problems:

First, your faith has been weakened, so that you lack the spiritual virility, vitality, verve and muscle which is necessary for standing in the time of pressure.

Furthermore, your withdrawal has put an extra burden on those who are fighting the good fight of faith; for not only must they contest the power of the enemy and stand against his onslaughts, but they must also protect *you* and fight *your* battles. They who are strong must uphold weak believers who are feeble and discouraged.

I say to you,
Rise out of your place of comfort.
Do not rest in the place of security and safety.
Rather, look at the world and understand that
your brothers and sisters in the faith are

valiantly doing all within their power to
represent their Lord in an unbelieving
world.

You must join them in the contest.

You must add your faith to theirs.
You must add your courage to theirs.
You must add your determination to theirs.

Instead of turning back
in the day of battle—
  go forth
  and fight,
  being fully armed
  with the armor I have given you.

Fight My battles with this watchword: "The Lord
is My helper; I will not fear what man shall do
to me."

Do not be a spectator
from the sidelines,
watching the contest.

Get into the arena.

The rewards are great for those who fight the good

fight of faith. I, who see in secret, will reward you openly.

Woe to them that are at ease in Zion .... (Amos 6:1)

A WORD FROM THE LORD
FOR THE AMBITIOUS

> *The kingdom of heaven is being seized as a treasure. The energetic, persistent, determined and fervent take it by force. (Matthew 11:12, paraphrased)*

The kingdom of Heaven
suffers violence,
and the violent take it by force.

It is the persistent,
    the determined,
    the energetic,
    the fervent
        who seize the prize.

I have much treasure,
        many prizes,
            many rewards,
                many hidden gifts.

hey wait—
>for the man who has determination—
>for the man who will seize them.

My kingdom can be seized.
>But I look upon the earth and see unconcern, apathy and smug indifference settling down as a power over the peoples of the earth.

But not you, My child.
I have touched your heart.
My Spirit has stirred you.

You cannot rest content in the realm of mediocrity. There is something stirring within you to seize the prize, snatch the treasure and possess the gift.

My treasure chest is open
>to the man who will seek Me with all his heart. I only wait for the ambitious, the energetic, the determined, the fervent seekers, to press on to the prize.

You know
>that much has been kept back because My people have not availed themselves of the oppor-

tunities I give. My Word has disclosed treasures untold, far beyond the imagination of any man—

> treasures
> treasures
> treasures
> treasures
> > which sound almost too good
> > to be true.

Therefore,
> do not shrink back in timidity.
> Do not hold back in false modesty—
> > but know that "it is I who am working in you, both to will and to do of My good pleasure."

I promise,
I will not mock you.
> I would not give you the ambitious desire to seize the prize, and then withhold the prize from you.

The very fact that I have given you this ambition to be filled with My fulness and to have My treasures is a clear indication that I will grant you the very desires of your heart and will give you that which will satisfy your soul.

Let no man condemn you.
Let none of your enemies accuse you.
Press on.

Do not be afraid
to launch out.
> Be brave enough to be a forerunner—a pioneer
> of new concepts. In seizing the prize, you will
> be an example to others; that which they see
> in your life will stimulate like desires in them.

My treasure is available for "whosoever will."

You have only to seek
and knock.

> In the day that you seek Me with all your
> heart, you will find Me.

*How long are ye slack to go to possess the land,
which the Lord God of your fathers hath given
you?* (Joshua 18:3)

A WORD FROM THE LORD
FOR THE UNAMBITIOUS

> *Ye have compassed this mountain long enough: turn you northward.* (Deuteronomy 2:3)

You
have
compassed
this mountain
l-o-n-g e-n-o-u-g-h.

It is time to move on.

In My goodness, I have
    granted you forgiveness,
    led you beside the still waters,
    satisfied the longings of your soul,
    brought you to a position of strength,
    filled you with the riches of My fulness.

But you have been sitting at the foot of this mountain of blessings— enjoying the beauty, the grandeur, the scenery— being grateful for your position and your peace.

You have stayed
at the foot of this mountain *so long*
that you have become inactive.

You have become *so comfortable*
that you want to stay
and not move on.

You have become *so familiar*
with the same patterns—
so acquainted with the status quo
that you lack the incentive
to gain more for Me.

I have much more for you: new horizons
                                    new vistas
                                    new conquests
                                    new dimensions
                                    new areas
                                    new goals
                                    new gifts
                                    new blessings
                                    new treasures
                                    new visitations.

But you lack the incentive to rise and press on. You have found a security in patterns which have become familiar. You have seen Me working in a certain prescribed manner. You have familiarized yourself with these ways.

You know where the enemy strikes.
Your life has become a routine.
You are familiar with the danger areas.
You are acquainted with the areas of blessing.
You are comfortable.

In your comfort, you are also at ease.
    Being at ease, you have become careless.
        In carelessness, you are being lulled to sleep.

    So I would say to you:
        It is time to rise
           from your ease
           from your carelessness
           from your comfortable surroundings.
        It is time to take
           a forward step
           a progressive step
           an advancing step
           an ambitious step
              to a new plateau.

Certainly, the journey will wind its way through unfamiliar territory, and you will face many new situations.

Nevertheless
> I, who have brought you thus far, will see you through. I, who have helped you in the past, will help you in the future.

This is My word:
> *You are not to lean on that which is familiar, safe, comfortable and secure; you are to lean on My arm, and let Me be your stay—let Me be your guide.*

> In this way, your confidence will not be in that with which you are familiar, but in My keeping power.

> *Arise ye, and depart; for this is not your rest.* (Micah 2:10)

A WORD FROM THE LORD
FOR THE APPREHENSIVE

> *Hitherto hath the Lord helped
> us.* (I Samuel 7:12)

This is your word of assurance for the future—for
the path that lies ahead.

You have had many anxious moments.
You have been inundated with doubts.
You have been fearful.

You are secretly tempted to believe that it
would be safer to retreat into the land of memories, into the nostalgia of yesterday, than to
bravely face the future.

But *hitherto* have I brought you—*hitherto* have I

helped you. This is the word you need for the future.

For I have not brought you this far to desert you, to leave you completely stranded, to let you find your way alone.

> I have begun a work of faith in your life.
> I have developed your Christian character.
> I have watched over your progress.
> I have supplied your needs.
> I have intervened for you.
> I have strengthened you.
> I have provided for you.
> I have protected you.
> I have delivered you.

Thus
> your confidence and your courage can be quickened by this thought: I have brought you this far—and I will see you through.

I did not bring you
to this place
> to forsake you,
> to leave you,
> to desert you,
> to abandon you.

I have brought you this far, that you might look
back and see
     how many times I have answered your prayers,
     how many times I have delivered you from
       danger,
     how many times I have protected you from
       peril,
     how many times I have provided for your
       needs,
     how many times I have poured blessings upon
       you,
     how many times I have given you guidance.

This shall be your foundation:
     "Hitherto hath the Lord helped us."

As I have provided for you in times past,
     so I will provide for you in the future.

As I have protected you in times past,
     so I will protect you in the future.

As I have preserved you in times past,
     so I will preserve you in the future.

"Hitherto hath the Lord helped us."
Say it again and again—knowing that I will yet
help you. Do not trust in the uncertain future—

but trust in My everlasting arms to sustain you continually.

... there is no restraint to the Lord to save by many or by few. (I Samuel 14:6)

A WORD FROM THE LORD
FOR THE GUILT-RIDDEN

> *If we confess our sins, he is
> faithful and just to forgive us our
> sins, and to cleanse us from all un-
> righteousness.* (I John 1:9)

I am faithful and just
to forgive all your sins
and to cleanse you from all unrighteousness.

Because of your guilt, life has no joy.
Because of your condemnation, life has no peace.
Because of conviction of sin, life has no refreshing.

You are weary with the heaviness of your guilt. But
you need not stand condemned and defeated.

There is cleansing.
There is forgiveness.
There is renewing.

You need not
repeat your confession of failure
  over and
    over and
      over and
        over again.

Come to Me.
Pour out your heart before Me.
Name your sin.
Confess your faults.
Acknowledge your wrongdoing.

Then look to Me
  as the Lover of your soul,
  as the Friend who is closer than a brother,
  as the Father who loves to bless His children.

From My hand, receive the assurance
    that your sins have been blotted out,
    that your failures have been removed,
    that your wrongdoing has been eradicated.

I have promised
in My Word
    that I will put all your sins
     behind My back.

But My back
is not as your back.
I am everywhere present.
I see all, hear all, know all.
I fill the heavens and the earth
    with My presence.

My back is My mercy.
  When you have confessed your sins to me—
    in *mercy*, I remove them out of My sight.
    In *mercy*, I remember them no more.
    In *mercy*, I do not remind you about them.

Once you have confessed these sins to Me, they are
blotted out. You are not to remember them, even
as I do not remember them. I have forgiven you and
cleansed you.

You shall have newness of life,
                  newness of joy,
                  newness of heart,
                  newness of spirit,
                  newness of song.

You shall no longer be downtrodden, with accusing guilt and condemnation. You shall be included among those who have been made free by the truth. You shall find the precious cleansing which is given to those who confess their sins and are cleansed by the blood of Jesus Christ.

There is therefore now no condemnation to them which are in Christ Jesus .... (Romans 8:1)

A WORD FROM THE LORD
FOR THOSE LACKING ASSURANCE
OF SALVATION

> ... it is the Spirit himself bear-
> ing witness with our spirit that we
> are children of God. (Romans
> 8:16, RSV)

You have shed your tears.
Now it is time to quit crying.

You have confessed your sins,
and I have heard that confession.
You need not repeat it
over and over again.

> Do not
> let yourself be hurt
> by much speaking.

> I heard you the first time.

Your heart was convicted by My Spirit, and in conviction, you cried to Me for deliverance. My word says, "Whosoever shall call upon the name of the Lord shall be saved."

But assurance has not come to you.
A cloud hangs over you—
a black cloud of despair.

You are caught in a web of doubt—
wondering if I have accepted you,
wondering if Jesus has really forgiven you,
wondering if My Spirit has really sealed you.

This lack of assurance does not come from Me.

No,
the enemy of your soul is trying to interfere with the joy I would give you— for it is My joy which is your strength.

He is trying to interfere with the peace I would give you— for it is My peace which keeps your heart and mind.

He is trying to interfere with the love I would give you— for it is My love which is shed abroad in your heart by the Holy Ghost.

But I say to you,
you must confess what My Word says— that you have come to Me, and that I will in no wise cast you out.

You have confessed your sins;
I have forgiven you.

You have named your transgessions;
I have blotted them out.

You have called upon Me;
I have saved you.

>Do not speak
>>words of doubt,
>>words of unbelief,
>>words that rob you of assurance.

Speak My promises; for none of these promises
shall fail you. I have given you these promises for
your assurance. Speak what My Word says. Declare
and decree and proclaim My Word. This is My way
of speaking to you. These are My words to you.

"Whosoever
shall call
upon the name of the Lord
shall be delivered."

>You have called.
>I have heard.
>I have saved you.
>I have delivered you.

I do not keep you at arm's length. I do not keep

you on probation— trying you, seeing whether you can meet certain specifications— before I will accept you.

No.
Whosoever shall call upon Me shall be saved. You have called. Therefore, you are saved.

The blood of Jesus Christ cleanses you from all sin. You were unable to cleanse yourself. But you asked Me to cleanse you— and the blood of Jesus has made that cleansing a reality.

In My eyes
> you are now clothed in garments of holiness
> and garments of righteousness.

> Your lack of assurance
> comes not only from your enemy,
> but from within yourself

> It is inconceivable to you that a loving Father
> would forgive you without you paying a price
> yourself.

"This is too good to be true,"
> you say.
"This is too much;
 surely there is something
 I must do."

You are tempted to believe that there is something you must do with your own hands— working for forgiveness, trying to earn it— not fully knowing that eternal life is a *free gift* for "whosover will."

> You cannot buy your salvation.
> > You do not deserve it.
> > You cannot earn it.

You can only receive it as My free gift.

Therefore
  do not punish yourself.
  Do not rob yourself
    of the blessing I have for you—
    the blessing which I would freely bestow
    upon you.

Does it seem too good to be true?
Nevertheless, it *is* true.
My mercy envelops you.
My mercy reaches you.
My grace is sufficient for you.

You can, *at this moment,* enjoy all My fullness and all the assurance I give. You can have the confidence of knowing that you are one of My redeemed ones— that you are My son.

It is God that justifieth. Who is he that condemneth? (Romans 8:33, 34)

A WORD FROM THE LORD
FOR THOSE HAVING DIFFICULTY
EXPRESSING THEMSELVES

> *... the desire of the righteous
> shall be granted.* (Proverbs (10:
> 24)

I will grant you the desire *of your heart*—
    that desire deep within you for which you can
    find no verbal expression.

I know
you have tried to express yourself,
                to express your feelings,
                      to describe your inner thoughts—
                         but have been unable to find
                         the appropriate words.

When you are alone,
    when you are relaxed,
        when you have no stress or strain,
            when you are in solitude—
                you can speak freely;

you can find expression
for your feelings.

But I also know
that when you are among people,
you are choked up.
You are unable
to put into words
exactly what you are feeling.

Even though this has caused you embarrassment—
even though you feel ill-at-ease among people—
even though you feel overly nervous and anxious
     when you walk into a large group of people—
even though it seems that your words are locked
     within you—
               still, I have promised to give you the
               desires of your heart— the words you
               need to communicate with people— the
               syllables needed to formulate expression.

Man looks on the outward appearance—
  I look *on the heart*.

     I know your heart, My child.
     I know your difficulties.
     I know your longings.
     I know your intense desires—
          desires which you have never been able to
          express in words—longings for which there
          are no descriptive phrases.

I, the Lord, am a heart-searcher,
>   a heart-reader,
>   a heart-knower.

I know your sincerity and your longings, even though words have been difficult for you— even though you have been unable to find expression.

I have promised to give you the desires of your heart. I have said in My Word, "Delight yourself in the Lord, and He will give you *the desires of your heart.*"

Be assured of this, that even though words do not come to you easily, I, the heart-reader and the heart-knower will reach forth My hand of sustaining power and grant you the desire of your heart.

> Then,
> when you see the desires of your heart fulfilled, your heart will rejoice and your mouth will speak forth My praises—for My mercy endures forever.

. . . man looketh on the outward appearance, but the Lord looketh on the heart. (I Samuel 16:7)

A WORD FROM THE LORD
FOR THE GIFTED

> *A man's gift maketh room for*
> *him, and bringeth him before*
> *great men.* (Proverbs 18:16)

When My Son ascended on high, He led captivity
captive, and gave gifts to men. These gifts I have
freely bestowed—freely distributed.

You have been the recipient of some of these gifts.
You have received that which I share
with My followers—gifts,
                    talents,
                        capabilities,
                        qualifications,
                    miraculous faculties,
                supernatural endowments.

Because of this
        you know that My hand has touched your life.

You are aware that I have given you direction, meaning and purpose.

My child, do not become enamored with your gift. Do not put too much focus upon your gift. My gifts and callings are without repentance. I did not give you these gifts because of human merit or achievement.

I gave them because

it is My nature to be benevolent.
It is My nature to lavish gifts.
It is My nature to freely give.

The greatest gift I ever gave you was the gift of My Son. I did this freely, because I loved you.

I have given you My Spirit.
I have given you rest.
I have given you peace.
I have given you eternal life.

It is My nature to give.

You have thought within yourself that you have a gift which is rare and extraordinary— a gift which is not often seen, and seldom given.

But beware—

set a guard over yourself, lest your heart be secretly lifted up with pride.

I did not give this gift that you might be destroyed
—nor to bring confusion to your fellow believers.

I gave this gift that you might serve,
                    that you might minister,
                    that you might flow out.

Therefore, My word to you is:
        Humbly depend upon Me.

The gift I have given you shall then
    bring rejoicing to many,
    bring blessing to many,
    bring inspiration to many,
    bring inward strength to many.

You will have the joy of being a channel of blessing.
You will have the joy of seeing Me moving and
working in your own life.

But you must give all glory to Me.
You must be in complete dependence upon Me.

Do not put your confidence in your gift; put your
confidence in Me, the Giver of all good and perfect
gifts.

   *Every good gift and every perfect gift is from
above ....* (James 1:17)

A WORD FROM THE LORD
FOR THE NON-GIFTED

> *So that ye come behind in no
> gift; waiting for the coming of our
> Lord . . .* (I Corinthians 1:7)

You shall not be
lacking in a gift,
as you wait for the coming of the Lord Jesus Christ.

You have looked at yourself and
wondered why your life seemed so barren,
                                    so empty,
                                    so fruitless,
                                    so unproductive.

You have even asked Me about this.
You have set your heart to seek Me.

    You are continually aware of those who seem
    to be more gifted than yourself—those who

have been endowed with the gifts of My Spirit. You have become spiritually introspective, comparing yourself with others. This ought not to be.

Remember how My apostle warned of those who are not wise, who measure themselves by themselves, and compare themselves among themselves.

I have set the members
in the body
as it has pleased Me.

I have distributed gifts to every man, according to My own will. Gifts of the Holy Spirit are distributed according to the will of My Spirit.

I know your capabilities.
I know your physical limitations.
I know the responsibilities you bear.
I know all that is required of you.

I have extended My hand of blessing to you in proportion to your capabilities. Some gifts that you have desired would not be suitable for you. Some gifts that you have thought to be outstanding in their power, their miraculousness, their great demonstration of My glory— would destroy you.

All gifts that I give to My people are tempered to each individual's capability.

Instead of looking within
and saying to yourself:
"I have not,"
you must realize that I *have* gifted you,
    according to your present capability.

> I have given you tasks to perform.
> I have given you a service to render.
> I have given you a ministry.
> I have given you a gift of helping.

Even though you feel that you lack the strength to stand and be a leader, yet I have given you the gift of helping.

With this gift, you shall augment,
                        minister,
                            add to,
                                aid, and
                                    assist in my program.

"The Lord which seeth in secret shall reward you openly." Use the talents I have already given you.

Exercise the gift of helping that I have bestowed upon you. If you do this, you will bless My body of believers.

For I long to see you, that I may impart unto you some spiritual gift .... (Romans 1:11)

A WORD FROM THE LORD
FOR THE EXTROVERT

> *Go in this thy might . . . have*
> *not I sent thee?* (Judges 6:14)

Go, in this your might:
  I have put a power within you.
  I have given you a determination.
  I have given you an energy.
  I have given you an outflow.

Thus,
    from your innermost being shall flow rivers o
    living water. You shall find a momentum—
    current—a tide of power flowing out of you.

Your life shall be one that is energetic and outflow
ing. You shall be as one who has something to give
for I have given you assurance,
                confidence, and
                humble boldness.

You shall go forth
in My power
and in My name.
I will give you
the courage
to rise above
all obstacles.

I will give you a mouth and wisdom that can neither
be gainsaid nor resisted. Even as Stephen of old was
full of faith and power, and did great wonders
among the people—and even as he spoke with such
wisdom and power that the people were not able to
resist him—so shall it be with you.

But
   you shall not go out with haste,
   nor by flight.
   I will go before you.

Stop.
Think.
Understand that it is I who am working within you,
both to will and to do of My good pleasure.
     I have given you your boldness.
     I have given you your fearlessness.

Therefore,
be cautious—
be careful—
     you must not act impetuously or impatiently.

You must not run in merely human strength.
You must not go in merely human power.
You must not lean to merely human understanding.

> But neither shall you be hidden,
>> or become indifferent,
>> or become inactive.

I have a work for you to do.
You have been stirred up by Me.
I have raised you up.
I have put My hand upon you
> that I might thrust you forth
> into a fruitful field.

I say to you,
> put no limits upon Me.
> Put no confinement upon Me.
> Put no restrictions upon Me—
>> for I am able to do above and beyond
>> all that you could possibly ask or think.

Therefore, know this—
> that because you have promptly obeyed Me,
> and implicitly followed My directions, I will
> bless you with even more courage,
>> even more strength,
>> even more power,
>> even more wisdom.

Your life and service to Me will bring praise and

glory to Me— and be a joy and blessing to you
throughout the coming ages.

   ... *the Spirit of the Lord came mightily upon
him* .... (Judges 14:6)

A WORD FROM THE LORD
FOR THE INTROVERT

> *It is more blessed to give than
> to receive.* (Acts 20:35)

This is My Word for you—
  for you are submerged in your own inadequacies,
  you are buried in feelings of insufficiency,
  you are downtrodden with spiritual inferiority,
  you have not felt equal to others.

But this is My Word to you:
  It is better to *give*
  than to receive.

If you will seek Me,
and draw nigh to Me,
I will reverse that within you which has kept you
submerged. I will give you the outflow for which
you have waited.

You have been looking to others
>to minister to you;
>to reassure you;
>to give you confidence;
>to give you courage;
>to show you the meaning of kindness.

You have wanted others to come to you—
but your direction has been wrong.

For, as others have come to you,
>they have made you feel even more inferior.
>They have made you feel even more insufficient.

But I say to you:
>I am going to do something within you.
>I am going to place My Spirit within you as a gift.
>I will cause My Spirit to flow out of your life.

You shall become an outflowing person.
Your direction shall change.

Instead of everything flowing into you, you will become an outflowing giver. You will say, "Truly, it *is* better to give than to receive." Out of your innermost being shall flow rivers of living water.

You will give
a cup of cold water—in My name.

If you are asked to go one mile,
you will go two.

If someone asks you for your coat,
you will also give them your cloak.

Therefore, look up.
I will raise your level in life.
I will release you from your imprisonment.
You will rise up and take your place in the sun.
You will be an outflowing person.
You will find great joy in giving,
                              in going,
                              in serving,
                              in doing.

For truly,
        it is *better* to give
        than to receive.

*I had fainted, unless I had believed to see the
goodness of the Lord in the land of the living.*
(Psalms 27:13)

A WORD FROM THE LORD
FOR TEACHERS

> *The Lord God hath given me*
> *the tongue of the learned, that I*
> *should know how to speak a word*
> *in season to him that is weary.*
> (Isaiah 50:4)

I have given you the tongue of the learned, that you might know how to speak a word in season to him that is weary. You shall be awakened morning by morning, to listen to My teaching.

Long ago
I said through My servant, Daniel, that knowledge would be increased in the time of the end. This was My Word to My people— a promise given to them for the latter times. But know this also, that even as there must be an increase of knowledge, in like manner there must be an increase of those who

101

teach knowledge. And you are part of the fulfillment
of that prophetic word.

Therefore,
> open your ears
> to hear what My Spirit is saying
> to the Church.

If you have ears to hear,
then *listen*:

> I will reveal Myself to you by My Word and
> Spirit.
> I will give you a revelation of My will.
> I will waken you in the morning hours.
> I will make known My truth to you.
> I will show you My mind.

> You will give this truth to others.
> You will teach others what I have taught you.
> You will share the knowledge I have given you.
> You will gain both natural and spiritual
> knowledge.

Truly,
> all kinds of knowledge will increase—
>> knowledge of the things of the world;
>> knowledge of things pertaining to Me.
>> *All* knowledge will multiply in the last times.

Therefore, know this:
> I am fulfilling My prophecies in you.

I am keeping My ancient promises through
   you.

Your speech shall be the speech of the instructed.
Your words shall have the marks of one who has
been taught by Me. I will give you an ear to hear.
I will give you a word to say.

As you go, I will go with you. I will give you knowledge and truth that is irresistible.

Look again to My Word—
   haven't I promised you that I would give you a
   mouth and wisdom which can neither be gainsaid
   nor resisted? Approach your task positively, with
   faith in Me.

   Do not teach, expecting to be rejected.
   Do not teach, expecting to be opposed.
   Do not teach, expecting to be repudiated.

I will not only give you some of My wisdom and
some of My knowledge, but I will also give you the
power of My Spirit, causing that which you teach
to be received—to be recognized—to be appreciated.

You shall be as My mouth.

   . . . *a word spoken in due season, how good is it!*
(Proverbs 15:23)

103

A WORD FROM THE LORD
FOR STUDENTS

> *Take my yoke upon you, and*
> *learn of Me.* (Matthew 11:29)

Take My yoke upon you.
Learn of Me—
>   for I am meek and lowly in heart,
>   and you will find rest
>   for your soul.

You are receiving instruction in the natural world.
You are acquiring much human knowledge.
I will help you retain this knowledge.
You will use it in times to come.

This knowledge will
>   enhance you in this world,
>   give you capabilities,
>   give you great possibilities,

> bring you promotion,
> > bring you achievement.

But
  I would also have you gain
  spiritual knowledge.

As you have received instruction at the hands of
earthly teachers, even so you must have a time of
waiting before Me, to receive instruction from Me.
I am your Heavenly Teacher.

So
  take My yoke upon you, and *learn* of Me.
  You will find rest for your soul.

  I have many hidden things to reveal to you.
  I have much knowledge to share with you.
  I have many doors to open for you.
  I have many treasures for you.

If you will only take the time to wait before Me,
I will give you much knowledge—
      knowledge of the holy,
      knowledge of the heavenly,
      knowledge of the things of the Spirit.

I have a word of knowledge for you.
  You must take time to wait before Me.
  You must let your spirit be still before Me.
  You must let your mind be stayed upon Me.

Even as you have gradually acquired natural knowledge, so I will give you spiritual knowledge as well. You will soon be well-informed about My ways.

Knowledge is easy unto him that understandeth. (Proverbs 14:6)

A WORD FROM THE LORD
FOR EMPLOYERS

> *... God is able to make all grace*
> *abound toward you; that ye ...*
> *may abound to every good work.*
> (II Corinthians 9:8)

Because of My abounding grace,
      you will have a ministry of generosity,
        you will be enriched in all things,
          you will have great bounty.

  There is a reason why
      I have given you these talents,
      I have led you in this particular pathway,
      I have given you employees,
      I have blessed you with this business,
      I have assigned you this work.

In so doing, I have opened up a great passageway
through which you can channel blessings to other

people. Your bounty and your generosity shall flow through this passageway, and I will use you to bless My people.

Thus
you will experience two wonderful things. *First*, My fullness in your own life— and *second*, My overflow that reaches out through you and touches others. And My blessings will keep you in this position.

Hear My Word again:
"The blessing of the Lord maketh rich,
    and He addeth no sorrow."

No man shall set on you to hurt you.
My blessings will protect you.

You are not dependent on surrounding conditions.
You are not dependent on current trends.
You are not dependent on the fluctuating economy.

Your success does not depend upon the conditions of the business world. Your business is not as other businesses, because *I am your Employer*. If I run your business, you can be sure it will succeed: I am not a God of failure.

I have given you all the gifts you have.
I have given you all the talents you have.
I am helping you utilize all these things
    according to My designs.

Know this:
>the more I do for you,
>the more you will be able to do for Me
>>in the furtherance of My program.

Therefore,
>impose no limits on Me.
>Put no restrictions on Me.
>Place no boundaries before Me.

I am able
to make all grace abound to you
that you may have sufficiency
in *all things*—
>and abound
>in every
>good work.

Thus you will become
>a channel of blessing for Me.
>>And in being such a channel,
>>>there shall be *no* limits
>>as to what I can do
>through your life.

*. . . and all goes well for the generous man who
conducts his business fairly.* (Psalms 112:5, Living
Bible)

A WORD FROM THE LORD
FOR EMPLOYEES

> . . . *the Lord blessed Obed-edom, and all his household.* (II Samuel 6:11)

Remember
how I blessed Obed-edom
and all his household.

Even David, the King,
heard of My blessings
on the household of Obed-edom,
because of the ark of the covenant
and My presence there.

I have given you a task.
I have given you a ministry.
I have put My blessing upon you.
    You will be as the ark

> in the household
> of Obed-edom.

The place of your employment will feel the impact of your faith, because you are My follower. Each of My followers is a treasure in My sight. Those who have left all to follow Me are endowed with a special blessing, even as the ark.

> I have caused a light to shine upon them.
> I have lifted a burden from their shoulders.
> I have delivered them from their guilt.
> I have saved them from their sins.
> I have translated them
> > from the kingdom of darkness
> > to the kingdom of light.

> They are new creations.
> They walk a straight and narrow path.
> They are blessed.
> They are to be envied.
> They have My touch.
> They have My favor.
> > as the ark.

No matter where you go,
no matter for whom you work—
> My blessing shall be upon you, and I will cause your employer to prosper; due to your presence there. I will cause My blessing to be upon the business because you have named My name.

Just as My ark dwelt in the household of Obed-edom, and everything in his house became blessed—became favored— became prosperous, *even so*, because you have come to this place of business, I will cause *it* to prosper.

Whatever you set your hand to do,
  I will cause it to prosper.

Wherever you go,
  I will clear the road for you.

Whenever you step out in My name,
  I will favor your righteous cause.

But know this:
      It is because of your faithfulness and devotion
      to Me that My blessing shall rest upon you.
            You must be responsible.
            You must act with dignity.
            You must represent Me
                  so that all
                  can see
                  My life
                  manifested
                  in you.

You are My witness in this place.

Because of you,
> I will bless all those with whom you work. They will know that My hand is upon you for good.

The blessing of the Lord, it maketh rich . . . .
(Proverbs 10:22)

A WORD FROM THE LORD
FOR THE OVERLY EAGER

> *Wherefore wilt thou run, my*
> *son, seeing that thou hast no tid-*
> *ings ready?* (II Samuel 18:22)

Why are you eager to run,
  when you are not prepared?

Why are you anxious to go,
  when you do not have the completed message?

In your impulsiveness and impatience, you are overly anxious. You want to run, but you do not have
the completed message— you do not have all the
details.

I know the beginning.
I know the end.

114

I look ahead.
I know what lies
    before you.

You look behind.
You see the past.
But you cannot see
    the future.

I know the future.
I know you are overly eager.
I know you feel ready to go.

        But you do not have all the facts.
        All the information is not in.

Just beyond your view are things yet to come to
light. It would be premature for you to run now,
for I have not yet prepared the way. You have not
yet reached your place of fulfillment and completion in Me. My work of grace is still being formu-
lated within you. If you should go now, you would
be going ahead of Me. You would be guilty of pre-
sumption.

I know your eagerness.
I know how ready you feel in your spirit.
I know your spirit is stirred, and is
    prompting you to action.

But I say to you,
>   do not run yet. Do not run until I give you the
>   complete tidings. Do not run until you have all
>   the facts and complete information.

>   *Then* I will activate you and send you forth.

>>   You will not be inactive forever.
>>   You will not be waiting forever.
>>   You will not be in transition forever.

Shortly,
>   when I have fulfilled My works in you—
>   when I have completed My design for you—
>   when you have received the completed
>>   message—
>   when you have received power for your
>>   ministry—
>   when you have received the release of My
>>   gifts—
>   when you have received My special
>>   endowment—
>>   *then*, I will do a quick thing,
>>   and I will thrust you forth.

When you go,
you will be a prepared vessel,
and your soul will rejoice

because you have waited
on Me.

*. . . the race is not to the swift, nor the battle to
the strong . . . .* (Ecclesiastes 9:11)

A WORD FROM THE LORD
FOR THE INDECISIVE

> *Stand ye in the ways, and see,*
> *and ask for the old paths, where is*
> *the good way, and walk therein,*
> *and ye shall find rest for your*
> *souls.* (Jeremiah 6:16)

You are standing
at a crossroad.
Two paths beckon you. You are in the throes of in-
decision. You are wondering which path you
should take.

One path beckons you with assurances
of security, safety and prosperity. It
calls to you, promising comfort, happiness and blessing.

Another path beckons you: a path of
sacrifice, of diligence, of devotion, of

118

toil, of effort— a path that bids you
walk in My strength, in My name,
doing My will.

One path looks so glamorous, so pleasant, so enticing— Something in you
would like the ease, the safety, the
pleasant surroundings of that path.

Be careful—walk in My ways. This
path calls you to nobler purposes. It
leads to fruitfulness and productivity.
It is a path of tears, of labor and sacrifice—with blessing.

Stand ye in the ways and see. Ask for the old paths.
These paths are not old because they are anti-
quated, outworn, outmoded, no longer relevant.
These paths are time-tested, time-honored and
time-proven.

If you will walk in these paths, you will find that
this is the good way, and your soul will rest content in Me.

Choose you this day whom ye will serve. (Joshua
24:15)

A WORD FROM THE LORD
FOR THE SICK

> *... I will restore health unto
> thee, and I will heal thee of thy
> wounds.* (Jeremiah 30:17)

My mission upon the earth was one of mercy and
compassion. I brought healing to all who were sick.
I am the Lord. I change not. I am the same, yesterday, today and forever.

> I have forgiven all your iniquities.
> I will heal all your diseases.

Seek out the promises of My Word. These promises
are My expressed will. I *will* heal you. I have sent
My Word to heal. My Word is still being sent forth,
still healing,
  still healing,
    still healing.

I know your infirmities.
I know your diseases.
I know your wounds.
I know your afflictions.

If you look to Me, My arm will be bared. I will
touch you. I will manifest My *life* in your mortal
flesh. The same Spirit which raises Jesus Christ
from the dead shall also quicken your mortal body.

> You can come to a new position of strength.
> You can find healing in My name.

Call for praying friends.
Call for praying elders.
Call for the anointing oil.

I say to you,
> "The prayer of faith SHALL save the sick, and
> the Lord shall raise him up."

My power has never been withdrawn from the
earth. My energy has never been removed. I am the
same, yesterday, today and forever.

If only you will look up, you will *live*.
I am the Author and Finisher of your faith.
I will give you LIFE to sustain you.
You shall come forth in newness of *life*.
You shall come forth in *resurrection life*.

You will say,

> "Truly, the hand of the Lord has touched my
> body. I have been healed by His power. I have
> been healed for His glory."

. . . with his stripes we are healed. (Isaiah 53:5)

A WORD FROM THE LORD
FOR THE REJECTED

"He came to his own, and his own received him not."

Therefore, be assured that I, your Lord and Master, know the pain of rejection. I came to bless, and My blessings were refused. I came to minister, and My ministry was scorned. I came to show a better way, and My counsel was ignored. I came to My own, and My own did not receive Me.

But know this: in your rejection, you are finding the rare treasure

of the fellowship of My sufferings.
If you suffer with Me, you will reign with Me.

Inasmuch as I was rejected, do not think it strange
that you are rejected also. The servant is not greater than his Lord.

I know your disappointments.
I know your anguish.
I know your grief.
I know your questions.

But,
I want you to know that I have a great blessing for
you. I have great treasure for you. I have a glory
to reveal to you. I have a Spirit to put upon you.

These blessings will more than compensate for all
your anguish and all your grief. You will enter into
a relationship of *intimacy*
with Me.

. As one who has suffered with Me, you will also be
one to reign with Me.

Blessed are you, My child.
Enter into the joy of your Lord. Share the fellowship of the suffering Savior. Share also the bless-

ings and rewards of identifying with Me.

Blessed are ye, when men . . . shall separate you from their company . . . . (Luke 6:22)

A WORD FROM THE LORD
FOR THE DESERTED

> *When my father and my*
> *mother forsake me, then the*
> *Lord will take me up.*
> (Psalms 27:10)

I look upon you,
and see the abrupt changes
which have come to you.

Once you had a family; *now* your family is gone.

Once there was a happy scene under your roof;
now you are sitting alone, as one abandoned and
rejected.

Once your loved ones were gathered about you;
now they are scattered and separated from you.

Once your home was a place of tranquillity and peace; now it is a place of loneliness and silence.

> Your heart is grief-stricken.
> Your thoughts are anguished.
> Your future seems bleak, without attraction.
> You are overwhelmed with grief and mourning.

These are My words to you:
> When your father and your mother forsake
>   you—
>   or a husband—
>   or a wife—
>   or a son—
>   or a daughter—
>   *then I* will take you up.

Am I not better than life itself?
Are not My ways better than your ways?
Are not My thoughts higher than your thoughts?
Are not My dealings better than human dealings?

> In your grief,
> and in your anguish,
>   *throw yourself upon My mercy.*

I will take you up.
> I will sustain you.
>> I will protect you.
>> I will love you.
>>> I will comfort you.

127

You will find a constant Friend in Me. I will be closer to you than any brother. You can rely on My promises:

I will never leave you.
I will never forsake you.
I will be better to you than a husband or wife.
I will be better to you than a son or daughter.

Encourage yourself by looking to Me.
I promise to sustain you.

I will be your dearest Friend.

He healeth the broken in heart, and bindeth up their wounds. (Psalms 147:3)

A WORD FROM THE LORD
FOR THE HAPPY

> *The lines are fallen unto me*
> *in pleasant places; yea, I have*
> *a goodly heritage.* (Psalms 16:6)

The lines have fallen to you in pleasant places. I have given you a goodly heritage. I have been good to you. In My goodness, I have extended mercies to you which have made you happy and serene.

This happiness
will be the means of touching others' lives.

You are surrounded by an unbelieving world,
  given to fear,
            pessimism,
            cynicism,
            despair,
            and gloom.

Your happiness will be conspicuous.
Your joy will be irresistible.

Many will come to you, inquiring about your free-
dom— your joy— your happiness. You shall say to
them:
   "The Lord has been good to me.
   I have received a precious inheritance.
   The lines have fallen to me in pleasant places.
   I have found all my sources of satisfaction
     in Him."

Many will recognize your happiness and your free-
    dom—
       the fearful,
       the anxious,
       the concerned,
       the troubled,
       the guilt-ridden,
       the disturbed,
       the down-trodden,
       the defeated
          will seek you out.

You shall tell them
that it is My goodness
which leads men to repentance.

Your happiness will be the means of converting
many people to Me. Therefore, rejoice in your por-
tion, and enjoy your inheritance. It is for this cause

that I have brought you forth, that you might be My happy witness.

Happy art thou . . . who is like unto thee, O people saved by the Lord . . . . (Deuteronomy 33:29)

A WORD FROM THE LORD
FOR THE FREE

> *Stand fast therefore in the liberty wherewith Christ hath made us free, and be not entangled again with the yoke of bondage.*
> (Galatians 5:1)

The p-r-o-c-e-s-s whereby I have reached you has been a sequence of events through which I have finally removed every chain that bound you and set you free.

You have been so familiar with bondage—
you have been so accustomed to confinement—
you have been so acquainted with restriction—
 that your freedom now seems too good to be true.

But listen to Me:
You must be careful.

You must consider—
  for the enemy of your soul would cause you to
  revert to a life of bondage. This is a constant
  danger. Reversion is all too easy. It is always
  easy to revert to the familiar—
                  the familiar bondage,
                  the familiar chains,
                  the familiar imprisonment.

But I would have you know freedom.
Not only have I *set* you free, but by My Word I
  would *keep* you free.

My Word gives you freedom of thought and freedom of expression. My Spirit *keeps* you free.
Through My Spirit, I will give you
        a life of prayer which has freedom,
        a life of worship which has freedom,
        a life of witnessing which has freedom.

Therefore,
  do not return to the life of bondage.
  Nor would I have you serve Me with compulsion.
  Let no man dominate, subdue or submerge you.

Walk in liberty.
Walk in freedom.

As you live in My freedom, you will help others to
find freedom. As you live in My release, you will

help others to find release. As you live in My out-flow, you will stimulate others to a life of outflow.

I have set you free
to walk in liberty,
n-e-v-e-r   a-g-a-i-n
to return to bondage.

If the Son therefore shall make you free, ye shall be free indeed. (John 8:36)

A WORD FROM THE LORD
FOR THE RELEASED

> *. . . he brought us out . . . that*
> *he might bring us in, to give us*
> *the land which he sware unto our*
> *fathers.* (Deuteronomy 6:23)

I brought you out
that I might bring you in.

You have surveyed all that I have done for you,
and you have been thrilled. You have rejoiced in
the wonderful release I have given you. Your life
has been changed. All things are fresh and new.

But I say to you,
   this is not the end
   of what I would do for you.
   This is but the beginning.

I brought you out of yourself,
  that you might walk in Me.

I brought you out of the flesh,
  that you might walk in the Spirit.

I brought you out of the world,
  that you might walk in My kingdom.

I brought you out of the works of the flesh,
  that you might walk in the fruit of My Spirit.

I brought you out of human resources and talents,
  that you might have the gifts of the Spirit.

Therefore,
be assured of this:
There is much growing to do.
You have not yet reached
fulfillment or completion.

I have many things to show you— many things to
give you— many truths to reveal to you— many
gifts to offer you— much goodness to share with
you.

I will show you things to come.
I will guide you into all truth.

You are not to stand still. Neither are you to go
back. I will lead you on to a land that lies before

you— a land to be possessed— a land full of treasures, blessings and gifts.

> I brought you out.
> I gave you freedom.
> I made you a new creation.
> I clothed you with My robe.
> I gave you an understanding of My mind.
> But there is more.

Seek My Word.
Be led by My Spirit.
> By so doing, you will be led to the fruitful place I have prepared for you.

When I begin, I will also make an end. (I Samuel 3:12)

A WORD FROM THE LORD
FOR THOSE AWAITING FULFILLMENT

> *For the vision is yet for an appointed time . . . though it tarry, wait for it; because it will surely come, it will not tarry.* (Habakkuk 2:3)

You have looked back, remembering the vision I gave you. With this vision came also an assurance of a work I would do in your life.

You have waited for fulfillment.
You have waited for the prophecy to come to pass.
You have waited long, wondering when . . . .

The enemy of your soul has tried to flood your mind with doubts. He has even suggested that you repudiate the promise I made you. He has suggested that you reject the dream I gave you— that you refuse the vision, casting it off as something spurious and unreal.

But
the vision is for an *appointed time*.
Even as My Word was given to Mary regarding those things I would do for her at an appointed time, so you must wait for the appointed time of your vision.

You shall have your performance.
You shall have your fulfillment.

I, the Lord, am the Author and Finisher of your faith. I authored the vision. I began it. And I will finish it.

In the meantime,
    I am preparing you,
            conditioning you,
            training you,
            disciplining you
                    that you might be ready
                    for the hour of My visitation.

In this time of waiting, I have shown you many things. I have developed longsuffering and patience within you.

Soon
    the time will come for fulfillment.

139

I, who have spoken to you, will shortly bring My
Word to pass. My promises will not be delayed
without purpose. That which I have spoken to you
shall be done.

*My covenant will I not break, nor alter the thing
that is gone out of my lips.* (Psalms 89:34)

A WORD FROM THE LORD
FOR THOSE TIRED OF WAITING

> *And it shall be said in that day,
> Lo, this is our God; we have wait-
> ed for him . . . we will be glad
> and rejoice in his salvation.*
> (Isaiah 25:9)

You have grown weary in waiting— waiting—
waiting.
You have grown tired.
You have grown anxious.
You have become fatigued.

You are carrying within you a desire which has not
yet come to pass. You have yearned and longed
many times to sit down,

to rest,

to discontinue your labor,

to cease to function,

to go in another direction.

141

But in My wisdom, I am leading you in the way you should go. I am guiding you in the paths which are best for you.

I know you have waited l-o-n-g.
The day is late.
The time is
short.

But there has been growth within your spirit due to this burden I have placed on your shoulders and within your heart.

> I have stood by your side.
> I have given you strength.
> I have given you wisdom.
> I have given you resources.
> I have protected you.

I have developed in you the ability to receive My grace in large quantities. While you were waiting on Me, I was enlarging your capacity,

> your grasp,
> your faith,
> your knowledge.

Now that you have been expanded by trials and adversities— and now that your heart has been enlarged, there is no more need of waiting.

You have become a prepared vessel.

There shall be no more delay.
You shall say,
 "This is the Lord.
  I waited for Him.
  He brought deliverance.
  This is the Lord."

You will rejoice in the great thing that I have done
for you.

   *Let not them that wait on thee, O Lord God of
   hosts, be ashamed . . . .* (Psalms 69:6)

A WORD FROM THE LORD
FOR THE CRITICIZED

> *Thou shalt keep them secretly*
> *in a pavilion from the strife of*
> *tongues.* (Psalms 31:20)

I will hide you
in the secret of My presence
from the pride of men.

I will
keep you secretly
in My pavilion
from the strife
of tongues.

You have been criticized.
The criticism has hurt you.
You have been condemned.
The condemnation has wounded you.

Others have questioned your motives,
        suspected your intentions,
        found fault with your actions.

But I say to you: I have a hiding place, even from
the pride of man. I have promised to hide you in
the secret of My presence. I have a place of near-
ness to My own heart, where you will be out of
reach of the enemy's assaults. I have a pavilion
where I can keep you from the strife of tongues.

There are those
who would lash at you
with their words.

But
I will touch your heart.
I will encircle your heart with My hands.
I will give you an immunity to criticism.

  Though people rage,
  though they rail,
  though they become vehement,
  though they become violent—
    still I will surround you with My grace.
    You will not be touched.

No weapon
that is formed against you
shall prosper.

Every tongue
that shall rise against you in judgment,
you will condemn.

This is your heritage from Me.
Your righteousness is of Me.
No man can set upon you to hurt you.
I, the Lord, have given you an immunity,
   even from the strife of tongues.

   Thou shalt be hid from the scourge of the tongue.
(Job 5:21)

A WORD FROM THE LORD
FOR DORMANT CHRISTIANS

For, lo, the
winter is past,
the rain is over
and gone; The flowers appear
on the earth; and the time of the sing-
ing of birds is come . . . . The fig tree put-
teth forth her green figs, and the vines with the
tender grape gives a good smell.

Arise My fair one . . . . You have been as one
hibernating. You have gone through the cold winter.
Seemingly, it has been a time of no activity. There
has been no fragrance, no bud, no blossom, no
fruit. You have been like a tree, shorn of its
foliage. You have been as one of My creatures, sleeping in a cave through the winter,
when everything is still, cold and quiet.

But all
this is
behind you.

The winter is past. The storms are over and gone. This is your Springtime. This is your resurrection-time. This is your time to emerge, to come forth in newness of life.

Even as the trees begin to get their new foliage, and the creatures end their sleep, now is the time for you to begin to produce.

You *shall* come forth—
    not as one who has been long dormant, lifeless and fruitless. But you shall come forth in *newness* of life. That which I do in your life will bring rejoicing to your soul.

You will be glad.
You will be one of My rejoicing ones who has been set free to serve Me in the fullness of My Holy Spirit.

Awake thou that sleepest . . . and Christ shall give thee light. (Ephesians 5:14)

A WORD FROM THE LORD
FOR LATENT CHRISTIANS

> *. . . stir up the gift of God,*
> *which is in thee . . . .* (II Timothy
> 1:6)

Do you not know
  that Deity resides in you?
  that My Spirit dwells in you?
  that you are the temple of the Holy Ghost?
  that My fullness resides in the Holy Spirit?

And in My Spirit resides all the fullness of grace,
all the fullness of fruitage, all the fullness of spiritual gifts.

Therefore,
 stir up that gift.

You have waited for a special endowment— a special visitation. You have waited for Me to bow the heavens and come down.

But I say to you:
"Greater is he that is within you, than he that is in the world. The Lord your God in the midst of you is mighty. He will inhabit your singing and your praise."

There shall be awakened within you your latent talent— your latent gift— that which has been residing in you, though not yet activated. It shall be brought forth in full strength.

You will behold Me
bringing forth from within you
> the wisdom,
> the power,
> the words,
> the knowledge,
> the faith,
> the healing
> > for which you have prayed.

All these things reside in My Spirit.
And My Spirit resides in you.

Therefore,
set your affections on things above.
Draw nigh to Me, and I will draw nigh to you.
I will help you stir up the gift that is in you.

Then you will go forth
in the fullness of My power.

Neglect not the gift that is in thee . . . . (I Timothy 4:14)

A WORD FROM THE LORD
FOR CHRISTIANS WITH
POTENTIAL MINISTRIES

> *Destroy it not; for a blessing
> is in it: so will I do for my serv-
> ants' sakes* . . . . (Isaiah 65:8)

The vine dresser looks at the vine.
With his natural sight, he sees only a twig.

But
with the eye of faith,
he sees the cluster that will be produced.

So let this vine grow.
Destroy it not.

You
    are as that twig in My eyes. I see you, not as
    others see you. I see you, not even as you see

yourself. When I look at you, I see the potential within. I see the Divine Gift which is resident in you.

When you look at yourself,
 you may seem to be only a twig.

Others, too, may not see your value,
                may discount you,
                may see no hope of fruitfulness,
                may see nothing but barrenness,
                may declare you sterile,
                may consider productivity hopeless.

Even loved ones and friends may not see in you any possibility of growth, development or fruitbearing. You may be only a twig in your own eyes, and in the eyes of your loved ones.

But I see new wine
in your cluster.

I will not destroy the twig,
for there is a blessing in it.

I will spare you
       that you may blossom forth—
          that your gift may be realized—
             that your potential may come to the surface.

I have been patient.

I have borne long with you.
In My love, I am cultivating and developing you.

This is My will for you:
> that you bear fruit—
> MUCH fruit.

When I look upon you,
this is what I see.

And let us not be weary in well doing: for in due season we shall reap, if we faint not. (Galatians 6:9)

A WORD FROM THE LORD
FOR NEW CHRISTIANS

> *As newborn babes, desire the
> sincere milk of the word, that ye
> may grow thereby.* (I Peter 2:2)

You have been born into My kingdom.
Your name is written in the Book of Life.
You are listed among the redeemed.
You will be among those gathered to My home.
You now have the name of Christ.
You have come out of darkness into My light.
You are a new creation.

Even as
 a baby comes into the world and must be cared
 for, so I will care for you— I will help you in
 growth and development.

Even as
 babies crawl and then learn to walk, so you will
 crawl slowly before learning to walk by faith.

Even as
> a baby learns to speak gradually, so you will learn to express yourself in worship, and share your faith with fellow-believers and the unbelieving world.

Even as
> a child learns sitting at the feet of tutors, so you will be taught by Me.

Even as
> a child reaches maturity and assumes adult responsibilities, so I will help you until you become a mature believer.

Look forward
with relish
to wonderful experiences with Me. I will communicate with you in prayer, in fellowship with other believers, and through the study of My Word. Truly, you will grow to be a mature, responsible, adult Christian.

Blessed are they which do hunger and thirst after righteousness: for they shall be filled. (Matthew 5:6)

A WORD FROM THE LORD
FOR ELDERLY CHRISTIANS

> *Thou shalt not be forgotten of me.* (Isaiah 44:21)

You are My servant.
I have formed you to serve Me.
You will never be forgotten by Me.

With precious memories,
you can now look back over your life,
and see that I have done great things
for you.

I have redeemed you.
  I have supplied your needs.
    I have blessed you.
      I have preserved you.
        I have protected you.

Now
  you are entering into the twilight of your life.

157

Your working years are behind you. BUT, be assured of this: I have begun a good work in you—and I will complete it. It will be gloriously consummated when I return for you.

You will not be discarded by Me.
Neither will you be neglected.

I care for you.
I know your burdens.
I know your concerns.

I also know the desires you have concerning your loved ones. Your family will be as a completed circle around My throne. They shall be Mine, in that day when I make up My jewels, and I will spare them as a father spares his own son.

Even in these latter years,
you will be fruitful and productive.

I know no age level.
My grace is for all ages.

> I say to you,
> I have begun a good work in you.
> I will perform it until My coming.
> You will be gathered to Me as one of Mine.
> You will enter into My joys.
> You will receive your reward
>   because you have faithfully followed Me.

... God is not unrighteous to forget your work and labour of love .... (Hebrews 6:10)

A WORD FROM THE LORD
FOR THOSE ASKING "WHO?"

> [*You shall be*] *satisfied with*
> *favour, and full with the blessing*
> *of the Lord.* (Deuteronomy 33:
> 23)

"The beloved of the Lord shall dwell in safety, and
the Lord shall cover him all day long."

With your eyes,
you will see Me make a distinction
between the believer and the unbeliever.

You will see believers bathed in light.
You will see unbelievers surrounded by a pallor of
  gloom, with an oppressive cloud over their minds.

My beloved
will dwell in safety.
You will see Me hiding, covering and protecting My
own. Have I not said that even in your dwelling
place I would give protection? Have I not said that

My name is a strong tower into which the righteous run for safety?

Therefore
you shall know that I make a distinction between those who are serving Me in love and devotion, and those who are rebelling against Me in resistance and unbelief.

Those who know Me
will be strong,
doing great exploits.

With your eyes,
you will see Me
making a distinction
between the believer
and the unbeliever.

Your own soul within you will tell you that those who follow Me do not stumble in darkness, but walk in light.

You will see Me protecting the believer. The disasters, the calamities, the destructions and distresses of life will not shake My beloved ones— for they have a secret not known to the world.

My beloved ones are hidden
in the palm of My hand.

I keep them safe.

... *there is a reward for the righteous.* (Psalms 58:11)

A WORD FROM THE LORD
FOR THOSE ASKING "WHEN?"

> *I the Lord will hasten it in his time.* (Isaiah 60:22)

I have a time
  in which I will manifest My power,
  in which I will show forth My energy,
  in which I will allow My purposes to be fulfilled.

You have become impatient.
You have become over-anxious.
You have tried to speed up the process.

But
My thoughts are not your thoughts.
My ways are not your ways.
I know what is best for you.

I would have you surrender yourself to My will. My
way is best. My way is perfect. There are no flaws

or defects in My dealings. I shall hasten it in My time. When I arise, the work of the enemy will be scattered. I will do a quick work in the earth.

Know this:
  You need not be anxious.
    You need not fret.
      You need not worry.

I will soon intervene.
I will stand between you and the power of the enemy.

The wicked shall flee when no one is pursuing.
But the righteous shall be bold as lions.

In that day, you will say,
"Truly, the Lord does all things well.
This is His day. This is His time."

You will rejoice
that you have waited for Me.
You shall see My great deliverance.

I will hasten it in My time.
My time is the perfect time.
It shall serve My purposes.
You will be joyful in it.

   . . . I will hasten my word to perform it. (Jeremiah 1:12)

A WORD FROM THE LORD
FOR THOSE ASKING "WHERE?"

> *Have not I commanded thee?*
> *Be strong and of a good courage*
> *... for the Lord thy God is with*
> *thee withersoever thou goest.*
> (Joshua 1:9)

"For the God of peace shall bruise Satan under your feet shortly."

But you have asked,
"Where shall the victory be,
O Lord?"

You have sought geographic locations.
You have wondered where you should be.
You know that I have victory for you—
   but where?

But I say to you,

My Spirit is empowering My followers
all over the earth.

They rise up, putting on My armor.
They shoe their feet with the Gospel of peace.
They tread upon serpents and scorpions.
They trample under foot the powers of darkness.

    And this is *your* heritage.
        This prerogative is *yours.*
        This sovereignty is *yours.*
        This authority is *yours.*
        This power is *yours.*

You shall tread under your feet the power of the
enemy, and you shall force demons into submission.
For I have made you more than a conqueror. You
are fully equipped.

Your victory can be accomplished in any place.
    You need only take My name, and use the power
    that dwells within you. My power (within you)
    will prevail against all the power of the enemy.

    Using My name,
      mentioning My blood,
        breathing My Word,
          being filled with My Spirit,
              you will tread on the power of the ene-
              my within your own home. You will see
              the powers of darkness put to flight,

and you will see the glory of the Lord
filling your household.

You will go forth;
and wherever the sole of your foot shall touch,
that is ground I would have you possess.

In going forth and putting down your feet, you are
treading on the power of the enemy. You are bringing victory to My cause—
wherever you are.

Fear thou not; for I am with thee. (Isaiah 41:10)

A WORD FROM THE LORD
FOR THOSE ASKING "HOW?"

> *Not by might, nor by power,*
> *but by my spirit, saith the Lord*
> *of hosts.* (Zechariah 4:6)

Not by might,
nor by power,
but by My Spirit,
   saith the Lord.

This is how you shall go forth.
This is how you will win your victory.

You have leaned
upon your own understanding. But your own
understanding has failed you. Therefore, *I* will
give you the Spirit of understanding.

You have run
in your own strength. But your strength has

drained away. Therefore, *I* will strengthen your spiritual man.

You have applied
your own wisdom. But your wisdom has not been sufficient. Therefore, *My* Spirit of wisdom shall rest upon you.

You have spoken
your own words. But your words have met with strong resistance. Therefore, My Spirit shall rest upon you, and you will speak the words *I* give you. You will then be irresistible.

Therefore, know this—
that in all you set your hand to do, My Spirit will empower you— and My Spirit will prevail against the power of the enemy.

My Spirit will work a miracle for you,
and glory and honor will come to Me.

Look not to your own weakness.
Look not to your own inabilities.
Look not to your lack of education.
Look not to your lack of resources.

Understand this:
My power is made perfect in human weakness. In your weakness, you will be made strong in Me and in the power of My might. Whatever is done

167

**will be accomplished by the power of My Spirit
in you.**

**You will see tremendous victory
wrought by My hand.**

Let God arise, let His enemies be scattered.
(Psalms 68:1)

A WORD FROM THE LORD
FOR THOSE ASKING "WHY?"

> *... in very deed for this cause*
> *have I raised thee up, for to shew*
> *in thee my power; and that my*
> *name may be declared throughout*
> *all the earth.* (Exodus 9:16)

I have chosen the foolish things of the world to confound the wise. I have chosen the weak things of the world to confound the things which are mighty. I have chosen the base things of the world, and things which are despised to bring to nought things that are— so that no flesh should glory in My presence.

This is why
I have chosen you—
>   that I might do supernatural things in your
>   life— things which will bring glory to Me.

169

This is why
I have chosen you—
> that I might work miracles in your life, bringing glory to My name.

This is why
I have raised you up—
> that I might display My power in you, and that My name might be declared throughout all the earth.

In all this, I, and *I alone*, shall be glorified.

You shall not glory in your pedigree,
> in your education,
> in your resources,
> in your position,
> in your achievements,
> in your accomplishments.

I, the Lord, will be exalted in My day, and that which man has done will be as nothing. That which I have done will fill the earth.

Know this:
> I have raised you up. I am using you. And I will continue to use you. I will do many more things in your life than I am doing now.

I am pleased with your desires— your consecration— your willingness. I rejoice in using you be-

cause you are not heaping the glory to yourself,
but glorifying My name.

Never forget:
I alone shall receive the praise.
No flesh shall glory in My presence.

But know this also:
  I will reward you,
  because you were the channel
  of blessing.

  ... *and the Lord alone shall be exalted in that
day.* (Isaiah 2:11)

THE FINAL WORD OF RELEASE

> *And now, behold, I loose thee*
> *this day from the chains which*
> *were upon thine hand.* (Jeremiah
> 40:4)

This is My word to you:
  You have been bound long enough. It is now time
  to come forth to freedom. You have had too many
  chains binding you for too long. My Gospel, My
  message, My words, are words of liberation.

While you were bound in chains,
        you were inactive,
        you were unfruitful,
        you were confused,
        you were imprisoned.

My truth sets men free.
My words liberate.

172

I speak to you
to rise for Me this day—
   loosed from all the chains which bound you:

the chains
   that were upon your soul which kept you in bondage—
the chains
   that were upon your mind which kept you from
   receiving the mind of Christ—
the chains
   that were upon your vocal cords which made you
   unable to speak freely in My name—
the chains
   that were upon your heart, so that you were unable to walk in faith and freedom before Me—
the chains
   that were upon your purse, which have restricted
   your funds and limited you, keeping you reduced
   to poverty—
the chains
   that were upon your spirit, which kept you dis-
   consolate and broken in spirit.

Your chains are all removed.
You have a new-found freedom.
You will demonstrate My freedom.
You are completely free.
You are ready to go forth.

Likewise, in your freedom, you will help many others to find the same freedom. In this way, My people will become strong. They will do mighty exploits in the freedom of My Spirit.

The king sent and loosed him . . . and let him go free. (Psalms 105:20)